Families Have Rules

by Cynthia Swain

I need to know these words.

dishes

family

homework

rule

This family has a rule.
The rule is, "Do
your homework."

This family has a rule.
The rule is, "Make
your bed."

This family has a rule. The rule is, "Wash your hands."

This family has
a rule, too.
The rule is, "Wash
the dishes."

This family has a rule.
The rule is, "Set
the table."

This family has a rule. The rule is, "Brush your teeth."

Do you have rules?